A Wonderful World
Beautiful and Bizarre Creations
Calm Coloring for Adults

By Edan Curtis

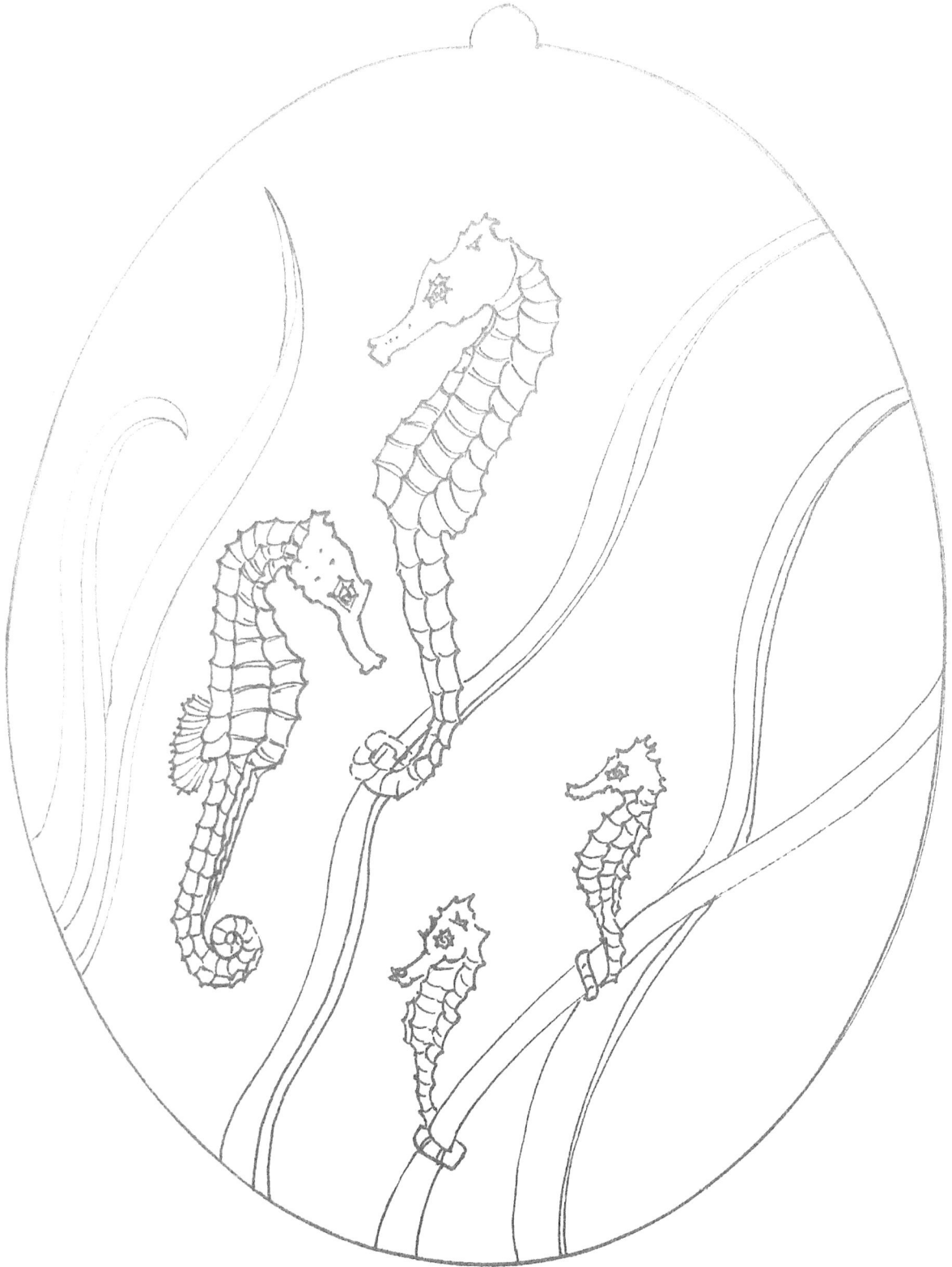

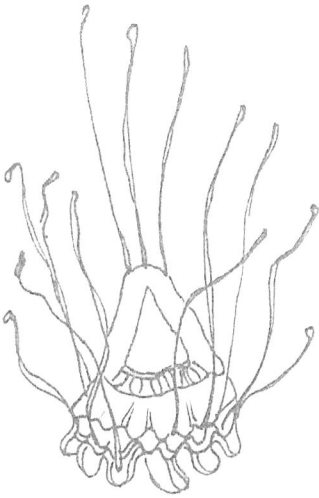

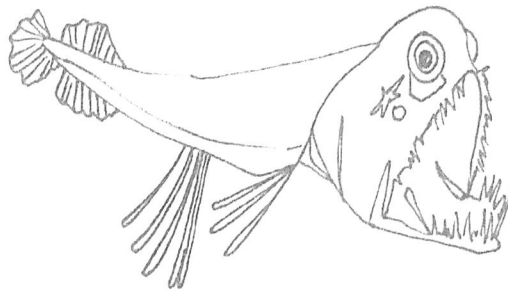

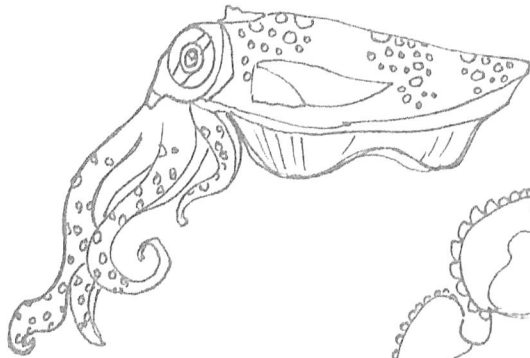

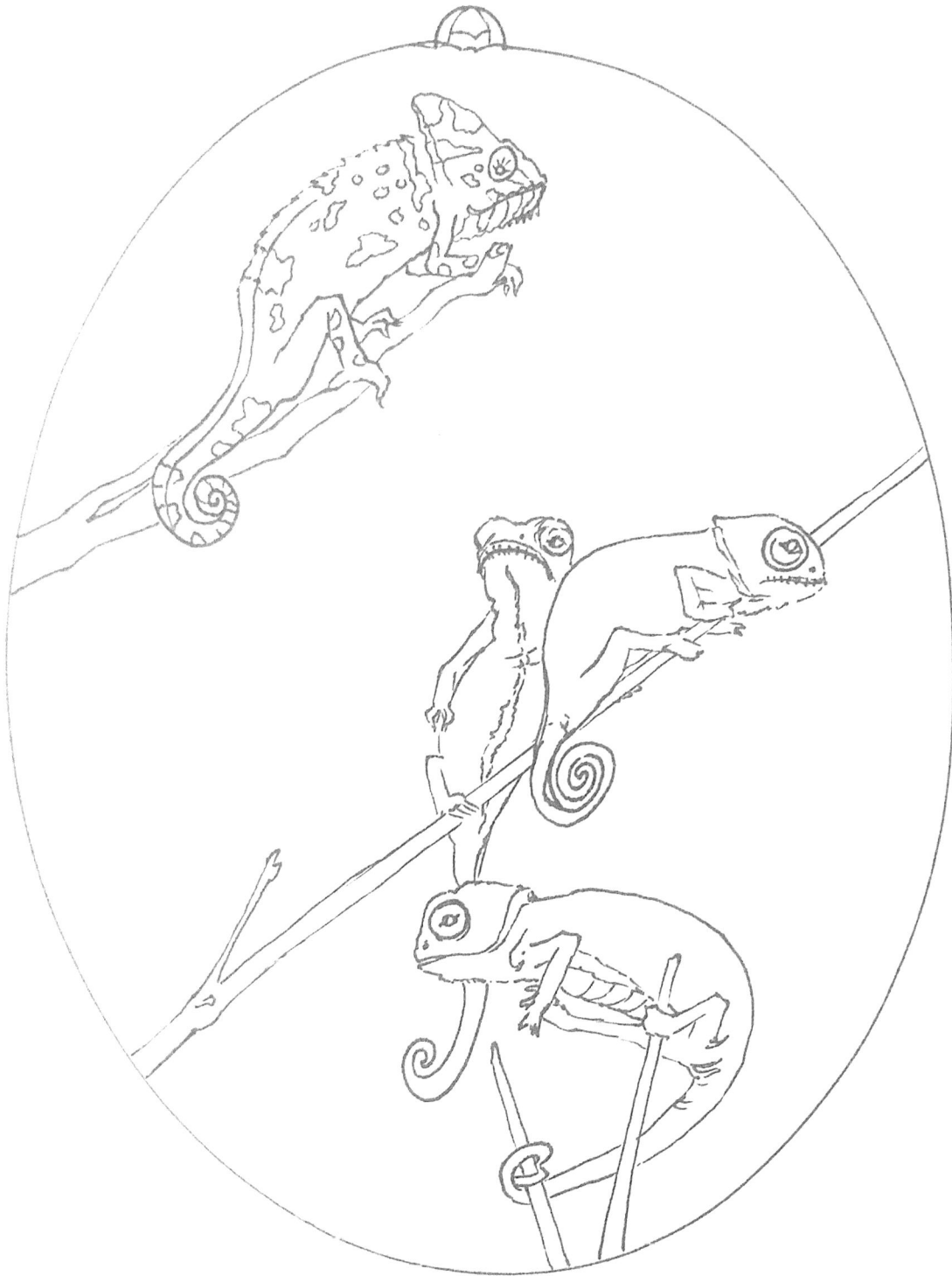

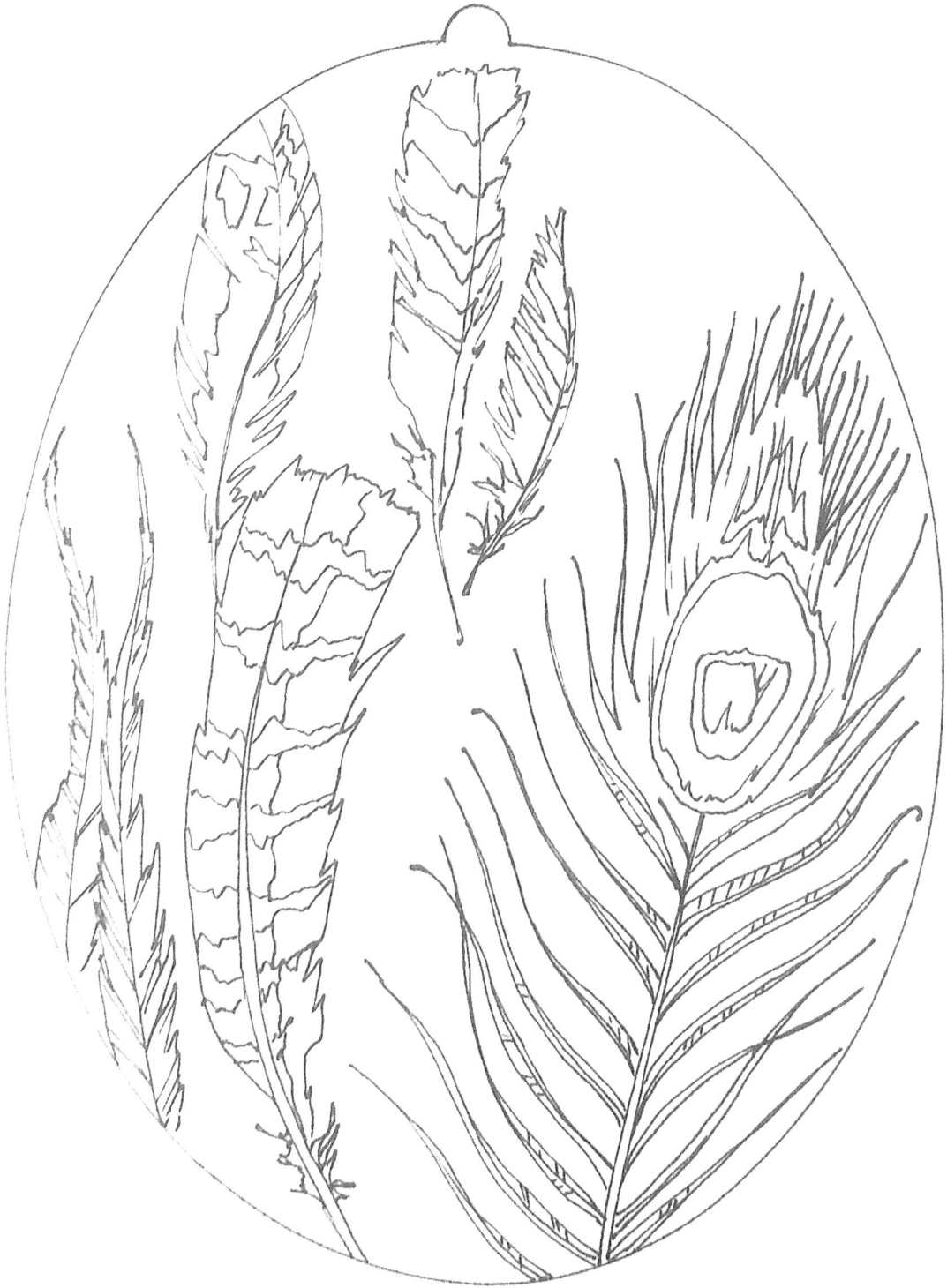

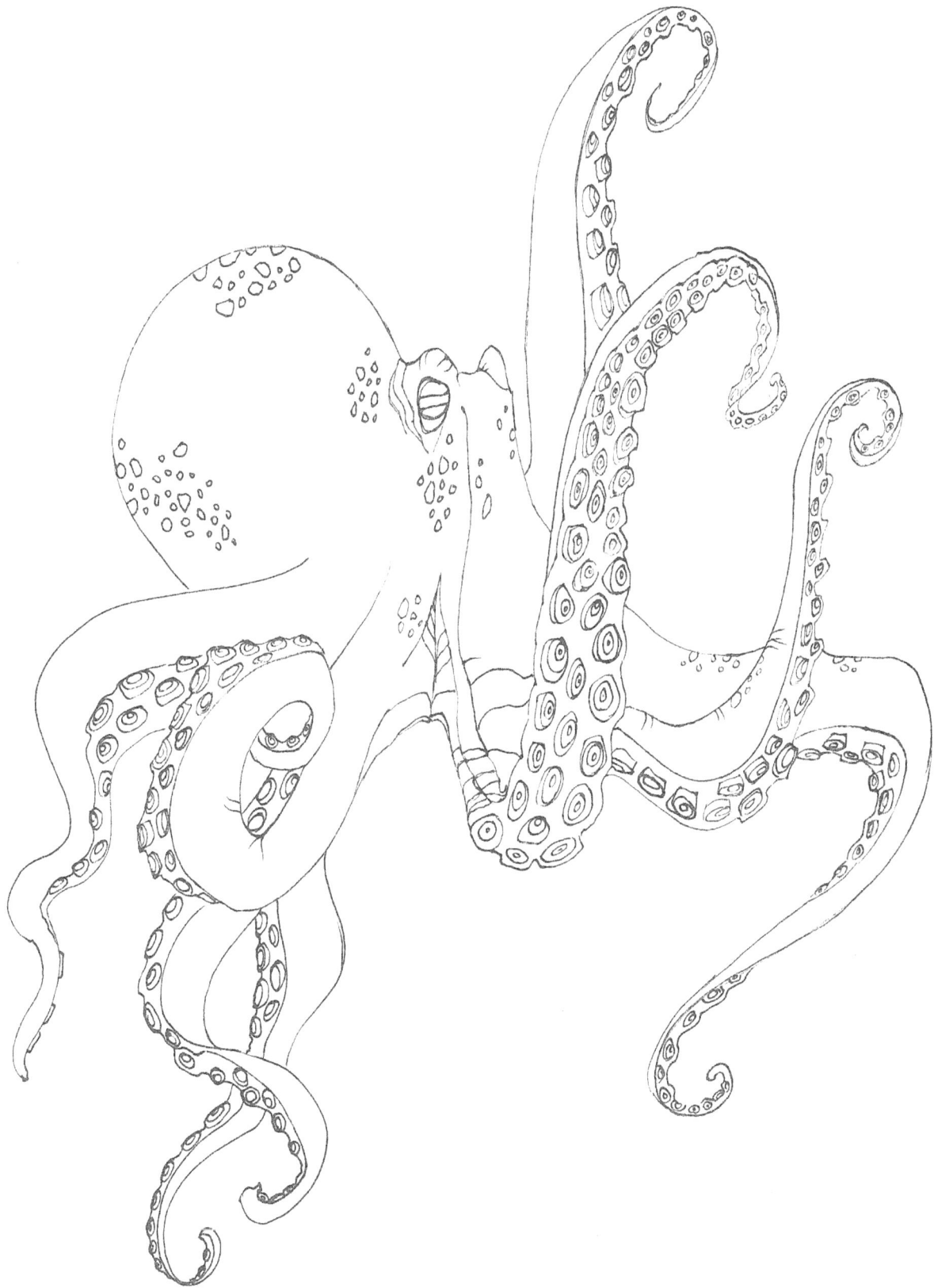

www.ingramcontent.com/pod-product-compliance
Lightning Source LLC
Chambersburg PA
CBHW081241020426
42331CB00013B/3259